Do You See Me?

Eliza Dreyer

BookLeaf Publishing

Presentation by *BookLeaf Publishing*

Web: www.bookleafpub.com

E-mail: info@bookleafpub.com

ISBN: 9789395950688

First edition 2022

To everyone who has never given up on me.

Autism is me

Autism and me, we often don't get along. We live side by side, but without one another we wouldn't belong.
Autism is my life, it's not an illness you can catch. It's nothing to be scared of, so please don't run or stare while I flap.
Autism is who I am and I'm not ashamed of that.
I'll tell it like it is and that is just that.
Autism, we're not all the same, nothing can change that, so please take a step back.
Autism is happy, it's jumping up and down, it's running around in circles, it's laughing like a clown.
When autism gets angry, it'll show it then and there. It won't hold it in, it'll stomp, scream and maybe swear.

There is nothing wrong with autism, it doesn't need a cure. It only wants acceptance and maybe a hug here or there.
Autism has friends, but sometimes others don't understand. Sometimes friends are invisible, sometimes we can't feel them with our hands.
Autism often smiles but sometimes smiles turn around. When someone asks me if I'm happy I often just look them up and down.
Autism confuses me; it confuses every cell; it makes me hot when it's cold or makes me laugh at a funeral.
Autism, it makes my feet feel weird, it makes me scream when my favourite socks have disappeared.
Autism, it's struggling with a book, it's looking out a window, it's learning how to cook.
Nothing says autism must conform to your ways. Let it live its life, let it rejoice in its ways.
Let autism be itself in its happy little way. You'll never see the world be so bright in every way.
Autism is amongst everyone; it hides in the shadows but then it triumphs and stands strong.
Autism is doing what I think is right. It's following the rules, it's not doing something wrong.
Autism, it loves to be alone, but sometimes it gets scared, so has to call home.

Autism, it has a heart of gold. It cares for everyone, no matter who or what they are.
Autism, it's a life full of learning, and it has a lesson to teach the world.
When autism gets started don't stop it in its tracks. Magic can happen, just believe me when I say that.
Nothing in autism is more important to me than that of having courage when others would have turned back.
Autism is taking risks; it's living for today.
Autism is standing strong, with courage, strength, and might. It's looking through the dark, it's waiting for the light.
Autism has many fears but never lets them show. It's trying a new food, or walking fast, then slow.
Autism has power; it wants people to understand. There's nothing wrong with autism, so let's stop shutting it down.
Autism is me, and I have accepted that, and I want the world to know. I'll make a song and dance; I'll turn it into a show. Don't shove me underwater, don't conform me to your ways. Let autism be itself, let me shine bright for all my days.

Laughter

Laugh starts with a letter
and ends with a smile
It creeps up inside
until it cannot hide
Your whole face turns red,
And you cry, oh so hard
What more could happen
when you're happy on every side?
Your sides start to ache,
And your face as well
You can't hold it in
Oh, what more could make you feel well?
It has the magic power
to turn your life upside down
Just a few minutes a day
and soon you'll feel swell
A joke with a friend
can soon turn into a puddle,
a blubbering mess

of tears, fun, and giggles
So, let's all gather around
Let's laugh till it hurts
We all share a story
Now let's celebrate another day here on earth

I am important

When people walk my way
I turn away
I run from fear
Of having anyone near
I'm terrified of what might happen
If I let someone in
If I let my pain show
People come and go
Some stay for a while
I even think some do give it a good go
But from my experience
I always end up alone
The regret it builds
My walls up tall
The darkness flows
It moans and groans

Because every time I take a chance
I start to take a step
Toward recuperation
And reclamation of my life
Someone new comes in
And there I am again
I let them in
And then soon
I feel like things will change
My life might improve
The pain might end
The celebration of joy of course
Then comes to an end
My walls are starting to fall
Slowly they crumble
They are being broken down
With kindness and care
But all this good will end
And soon enough
My walls will be tall again
I let you in and I held you close
You swore you would never
Relinquish your post
I trusted you
And now I'm alone
It's dark in here all over again
Why do I keep forgetting the end?
Why does my pain always win?
Why do I never seem to know?

How things will go
It's always the same
It will never be distinct
This story will continue until my end
The pain will build
My walls are forever tall
But then I will meet someone
New once again
And just like before
My defences will crumble
My heart will be on show
For all to see
For all to know
Don't destroy me anymore
Teach me to trust
That no matter what
You won't let me go
That there are people out there
Who truly do care?
That'll help me through
That'll show me my worth
And never let me down
I need to trust that this is you
I need to know how this will go
If you'll let me down
Please just go
I cannot live through another show
I need a place
Where I am safe

Where my comfort
And dignity is not for sale
I want a place where I can go
To be safe and secure and always know
I am cared for no matter what
That my life is important
And my opinion matters
I want to know that I matter
Please help me to know
That Once and for all
I am important
And my life is meaningful!

Little spark

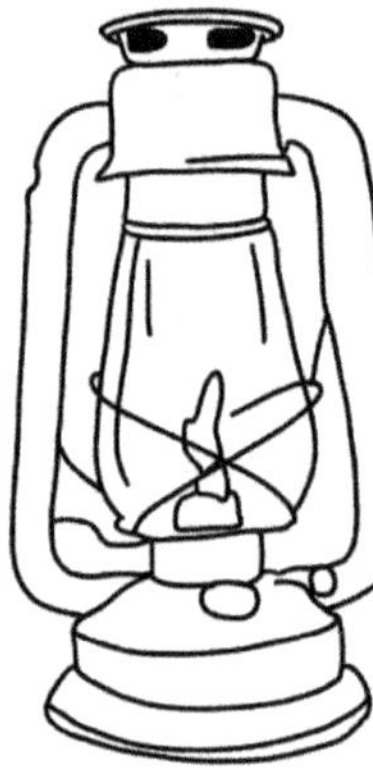

Living for today
That's what I really want
I wish that I was happy
And to never get left out
To always run-in freedom
To never look behind
All I ever wanted
Is to be secure
And safe as well
I want to look around and see
A world that's happy to see me
Only smiling faces
Never grumpy frumpy people
The grass always seems greener
On the other side

And the sun seems to shine much brighter
Over the wall far away
But never forget your purpose
Your courage, strength, and fight
Your willpower will be your saviour
It'll push you through the night
Your care for every person
Is truly an incredible sight
I want you to forever remember
This is our favourite part
We love your sense of humour
Your little childish quips
Your jokes and wicked smile
Light up the entire house
Never change for anyone
We would lose you precious one
And that would be disastrous
The world would soon go dark
You bring the light to everyone
Our precious little spark

Can you see me now?

Do they see beyond my eyes?
Into the world that lies on the inside
Where courage sinks and fear takes hold
Does anyone know how it really goes?
They only see what they want to believe
No one understands what it's like to be me
I'll run in circles but don't judge me
I'm living my life like I need it to be
From crashing waves of fear and shame
To tsunamis and cyclones of anxiety
People just don't get my life and me
They only believe what they want to see
I'm drowning in a puddle of sweat
I'm terrified and full of regret
Then I wonder will I be free
From this life that has consumed me

I’ve grown up wearing this mask
Now no one can tell us apart
I want to live not just survive
I want to be me for everyone to see
The time has come to take a stand
I’ll hold my head high I won’t back down
To live for myself and not let others decide
My life my way, the way it should be!

Forever okay

I’m done tonight
I’ve fought for my life
I’ve tried my best
I’m ready to die
When the pain inside
Flows out your eyes
When you run and hide
And you’ve got nothing inside
You’ve fought a good fight
Now it’s time to say goodbye
Nothing matters
Nothing is worth a try
No more tonight
I’m done I'll cry
I’ll cry until my eyes are dry
Until there’s nothing left inside
The pain it throbs

It aches and spins
I need it to end
That's all I can defend
I'm empty within
I've died inside
I've got no smile to show
I feel like I've been buried in snow
My heart is old
My bones are cold
Just let me go
Like the passing wind
You will hear a chime
As my time flies by
A drifting space
This time and place
Pain clouds my brain
Like a fog is shifting
Around my memories
Nothing left in sight
No survivors to be seen
I'll soon be near
My forever tears
And just like that
Life snaps me back
To the reality that I hold dear
With forget me nots
And hugs a lot
Pain-free and free from fear
I'll sigh again

And remember then
The dreams I have
Although so near
Are only there to keep me near
Here to stay forever okay

Jumping through hoops

Jumping through hoops
Running through fire
Spinning and twisting
Oh, what more is required
I can speak for myself
So don't shut me down
I can tell you my story
I don't need a hand
I don't need your help
I can yell oh so loud
I'll scream in your face
Until you back down
Don't carry me around
Don't baby me
I don't need your pity
I just need some time

Please listen to me
I can talk for myself
I have words and have courage
So please just sit down
Listen don't talk
Take notes don't say putdowns
Ask questions so you understand
And then respect me for who I am

My house is my home

My house is my home
And that's special to me
My home is my sanctuary
And that's how it should be
I have control of every little thing
So don't touch my stuff
Without asking me, please
If my tables a mess
That's okay with me
I like it that way
Don't tell me how it should be
I like my home exactly as is
With magnets on the fridge
And a swing on the balcony
My couch is just right
It's comfy you see
My tv stays off
And that's good with me

There're plants everywhere
And bread baking to see
There're soft toys galore
And dog toys as well
My wardrobes are packed full of all crafty things
Like fabric and cardboard
Vinyl and string
I will decide how my home is to look
You see It will not be all clinical
Or straight from a book
It'll be full of love, self-expression
Art, craft, and family
I'll have paintings on the walls
And also, coca cola collectibles
The bookcases will be filled
With All things special to me
There will be photos all around
Of past memories
And my home will be my haven
To create the life that I need
You won't be welcomed in
If you do not agree
That my house is my home
And it's only for me!

Don't be a puppet

Live like you want to
Don’t let others decide
Don’t be a puppet
Dead on the inside
Don’t dangle from strings
Don’t sit and do nothing
Don’t hide in the closet
But have fun in the world
Dance with no purpose
Have fun for yourself
Play games with one another
Live life like no other
It’s your time to shine
Show the world your bright light
If nothing else matters
For adventure is hindsight
Take one day at a time

And don't dwell on the past
Live life with excitement
But most importantly shine!

I am unique

My world and my way
Is special to me
I am unique
In every single way
From my walk
To my talk
From my smile
To my song
Don't pressure me to change
Don't make me be the same
Don't make me follow
Don't conform me to your ways
Let my laugh become contagious
Let my smile sweep the world
Allow me to spread my wings and fly
Don't hold me back in any way
Let me repeat it again

I'll scream it oh so loud
I'll sing it from the rooftops
I'll whisper it in every ear
I'll never let my message die
My purpose may be different
To you or you or you
But never underestimate
The strength
The Courage
The pride
Or the love
All that are deep inside
I am not broken
I do not need fixing
I am not a project that you work on every day
I am unique
I am special
I am worthwhile
And nothing can ever take that away

Never forgotten

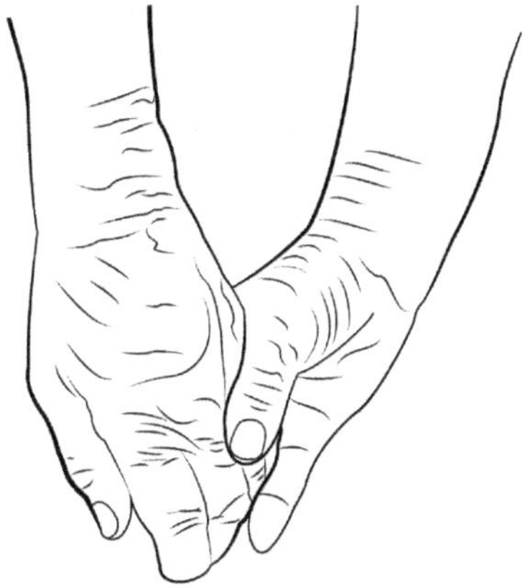

Sometimes when the body gets old
The muscles get tired and weak
The mind might no longer be at its peak
And sometimes all they can do is sleep
When the end is finally near
There won't be a dry eye anywhere
But when all is said and done
We will never be apart again
Don't cry for me my dears
I no longer have any fear
My soul is at peace
I am no longer weak
Their hearts have been set free
They now have angle wings
Forever they will look over our shoulders
Forever guiding us through our tears

We will never forget their love
Even when our hearts ache
We will remember them forever
In our hearts and minds
The memories are so clear
The smiles hugs and laughs
The days spent with them
Never forgotten but cherished with love

Pain

The pain it taunts
It twists and spins
It forces you
To do unusual things
You scream and squirm
You cry till you break
The sounds you make
How could this possibly be fake
You hear them grumble
You hear them moan
You want it to end
All you want is to go home
The pain inside
Is a big dark fog
It clouds your eyes
Until you explode inside
Till the time
When you push through
I'll guide you home
I'll keep you sane
Just keep strong
And don't give in

You will get there
The pain won’t win

Morning is here

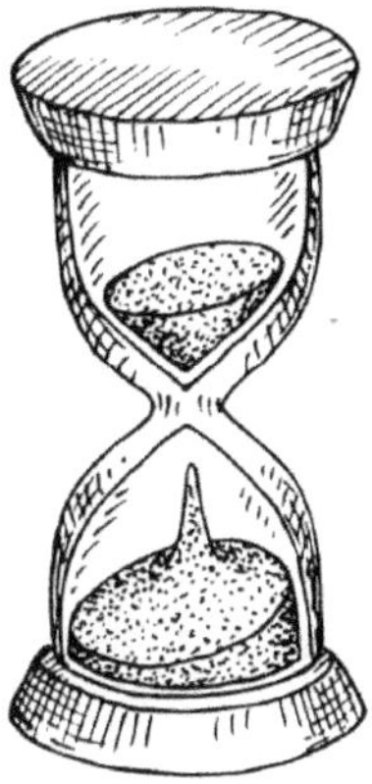

Please hold my hand
And don't let go
I'm terrified I hope you know
Please lead me through
And always know
That no matter what
No matter where
I'll always be
Standing there
I'm right behind
Just turn around
I need you to know
That no matter who
Comes and goes
The light will shine

And guide the road
So don’t give up
And just push through
The night will turn
To daytime soon
So never fear
My darling dear
Your closer to home
When you stand here
You’ve fought to win
Through pain and sin
There’s no more fear
The morning is here

Beautiful life

I love to look around
And see the sights and sounds
The smell of the grass
The breeze through my hair
There's nothing more to wish for
I'm bobbing over the waves
I'm flying way up high
The thunder and the rain
That makes way for the shining sun
The rainbows peeking through
My world is so much fun
The sand beneath my feet
That warms my cold sad soul
I've never felt so happy

Then when I'm jumping
Puddles with mum
The warm food in my belly
The cool drink in the sun
The candy and the crisps
Oh, how I love the life I'm living
Yes, some days are dark
But I try to not forget
That my life is so much better
Then many others will ever get
So, then I look around me
And I see the smiling faces
And I say thank gosh and thank heavens
For this life, I have been given

Silly little stone

One day a skipping stone
Sang a silly little song
It went plip plop plippidy plop
Until one day it was forced to stop
The poor little stone
Was forced to hide away
Because its silly song
Was too happy to see the light of day
Then the skipping stone
Thought why should I listen to them
My silly little song
Makes everybody's day
So, when you skim a little rock
Remember to laugh and play
For that little plippidy plop
May soon be gone away

Autism to me

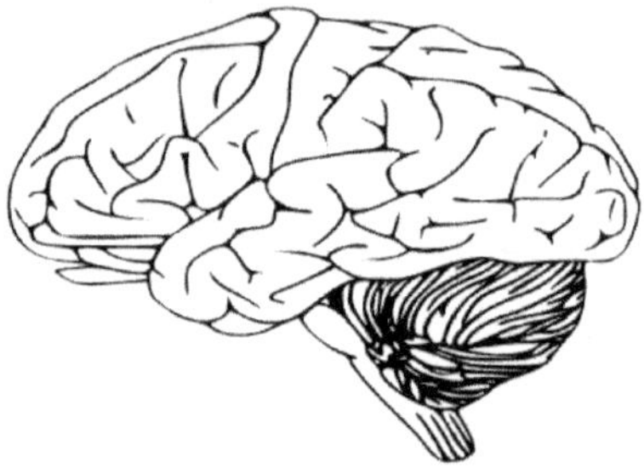

Autism to me it's how my life is
I hope to explain so that others might gain
An insight into my brain
I live with autism but it isn't a curse
I'm still a human being I still have worth
My lifestyle might be different
And my choices might seem strange
But if you give me some time
I'll try to explain
Sometimes my socks
Simply don't feel right
Sometimes I have to take them off
Otherwise, my emotions go POP
When people put their fingers together
I get sick on the inside
I might even vomit for real every once in a while
When people touch me

I get shivers down my spine
It makes me feel pain
And sometimes I might exclaim
I can't read people like others can do
I might not understand things like you to
When people make jokes, I'm never sure if they are true
I sometimes wish I knew things like how to chew
My senses might be different
To my neurotypical palls
I often don't feel pain until I'm overwhelmed
And I get hot really easy even when it's blowing a gale
Sometimes I look around and I notice little things
Like the sign on a corner three blocks northwest of the bell
When others try to tell me just how well I am doing
I don't know how to answer
I just nod and think can't they tell
My brain is in pieces my emotions are a wreck
I only want to curl up and sleep well, what the hell?
Why do people act like they know?
Why do people tell me I'm too slow?
I live in fear of not living up to the game
Of failing in every aspect of my brain

I just want to be seen and understood as well
I wish I was free I want to be released from my hell
Nothing makes me happier
Then when I am safe
Curled up in a swing living at my pace
If my life is too slow, I am sorry you know
But it's my life and my space
Not yours to control
So, let's take a step back
And let's see things my way
I want to be seen I want to be free
My life is not a shame
I am simply unique in my way
So, let's understand that although I might have autism
I still deserve to live however I wish

Passion project

Around and around, we go
Every stitch and every row
Count them twice just to be sure
You don't want to be short
The hook goes through
And pulls the yarn back
Then it's looped and pulled through again
First the body
Then some legs
One arm than two
And of course, the head
You stitch the eyes
And a cheeky grin
You even crack a smile back at him
Every stitch is done so tight
People say wow what a sight
I work so fast

And for so long
To make the toy good and strong
Then on the stall
The cheeky thing goes
To be bought by the woman
When it makes her smile
She lets me know
That soon it'll go
On a plane and over the seas
To a baby who has just greeted the world
I'll smile and say enjoy your day
And in my heart
The fireworks start
Because I know
That my crochet
Has a new home
Where it will be cherished
With years of love
And that's the dream
For my passion to be seen

The world is my playground

The world is my playground but many don't believe
They don't see things the way I perceive
I get told over and over that this life is a disease
They don't understand me and my routines
Some people try hard to make my life change
They take me to therapies to try and change my brain
They don't understand that I am a gift
They only want to make me fit
But I have a message to yell loud and clear
I'll tell it like it is by every means I can
You see my voice may be silent but that is not the only way
I'll write it, I'll sign it, I'll get my message to you today

Don't treat me like an illness, I am here to stay
My life, my methods I am unique in every single way
I may be on the spectrum but that doesn't mean I'm less
I'll put you in the dustpan on every single test
I'll run circles around your focus and burn past you in crochet
You see the things you take for granted and assume I don't have
My empathy and courage, my caring nature, and my love
I am a deserving person, I do not need to change
The world needs to learn that although I have autism
It's not my entirety I still deserve the best
So next time you are near
Why don't you take a look so you can see clearly?
My life might need structure and routine
But never underestimate
I will be important just you wait
One day you will need me and my ways.

Hanging on

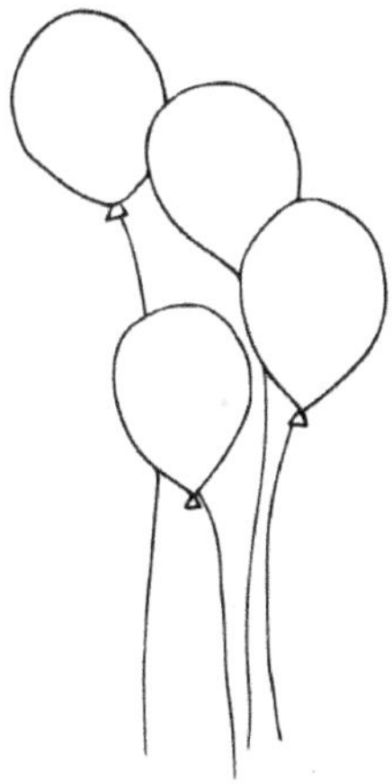

Tonight, I lay beneath the stars
I look back on dreams of past
I scream inside with the pain I hide
No more tonight I'm done I tried
The pain inside is a big dark fog
It fills up my soul Until I lose control
The pain I feel flows out my eyes
The choice I make will change my life
Do I float away in a bout of pain?
Or do I just hang on and try to stay sane
The choice I make will determine my fate
I look around and see the green
The grass the leaves and the big old trees

Then the yellow of the daisies swaying in the breeze
The sky is blue and the clouds are white
I listen to the bird calls and I begin to marvel
That This life might actually be all right
the pain inside I no longer must hide
I can look forward to the future
The past is the past now Don't forget to let go
I will take that leap and I will get through

Every year on Christmas

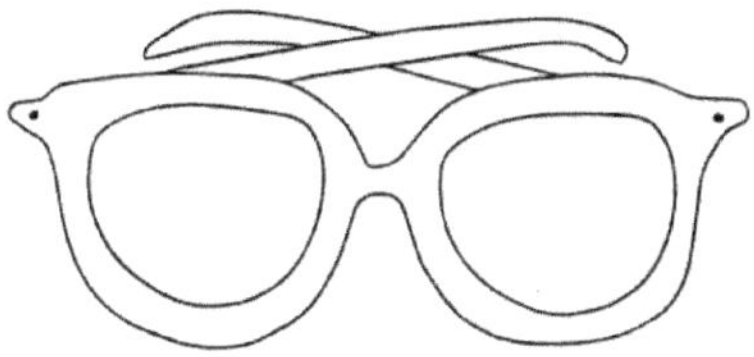

Every year on Christmas night
When I turn in for bed
The thoughts that run through my head
About everything I've given, done, and said
Did I smile in the right way
When people said g'day
And was my hug tight enough
Or did I squeeze them within an inch of their life?
Was my laugh too loud?
My handshake too strong?
Was everything I did
Simply wrong?
The gifts I've given were they okay
Or did I come on a little strong
Did I spend too much time
Playing on my phone
Was I talking enough to everyone?

Did I play the games right
Or did I play them to well
I'll never understand how to make Christmas go swell
So, every Christmas eve I make a wish
before I climb into bed
I ask that this year be a special year
And that Santa might bring me just one gift
A gift to help me understand
A gift to keep me strong
A gift that'll keep me simply plodding along
A gift to make Christmas not so long
I don't need it wrapped in fancy paper
Or tied up with a bow
I need it in my heart
I need it somewhere so that everyone knows
Christmas is not for everyone
There are many just like me
Who struggle with the festive season
For many more reasons than you would believe
So today as I write I ask for this, please
Look into your hearts
And accept me for me
For us as we are
Not whom you want us to be
Now let's enjoy Christmas
In our own special way
Let's stop the expectations
and all have fun in our ways

Thank you

I'm sorry for the ones,
That I have turned away
That only tried to help,
And gave me a shoulder to cry on,
In every single way
I know that I am selfish,
And that I need to change
So, help me, lord,
In your loving way
Give me guidance, strength, and courage,
To never shy away
From the ones who love me
And who are here to stay

In my dreams I see them,
Every single night,
The ones who fought but lost,
In this big ugly fight
Thank you, Lord, for showing me,
What it truly means,
For others to have faith in me
Who want to see me win
I know that one day
I'll throw the knockout punch,
To this world that has consumed me
For its very own lunch
My body tells a story,
My arms, my stomach, and my legs
The scars may never fade,
But I'll tell you one thing that did
Depression and other things
Yes, they took a hold,
They even held on tight
When the tide began to roll
They forced me underwater
Tried to make me hold my breath
But one thing they didn't count on
Were others who came around
No matter how hard I tried
No matter what I said
It didn't change their minds on me
They told me I was not dead
Some days my life is dark

Others, let's just say there worse
But then, sometimes
Life has its little perks
Like playing with a dog
Or listening to the rain
Or running down the street
Tryna catch a train
When I do those things
And many others as well
I remember, hell
I'm alive and well
So, thank you, everyone
Who has ever been involved
Whom I have tried to push away
But always stuck around
I now know that one day
My life will soon be good
I'll achieve my many goals
Because people understood
It's all because of you
That my dreams came true
I WILL get well
And I know it's because
You will help me through

www.ingramcontent.com/pod-product-compliance
Lightning Source LLC
Chambersburg PA
CBHW051739130826
49812CB00033B/925
* 9 7 8 9 3 9 5 9 5 0 6 8 8 *